THE

CRAP
EXCUSES

THE LITTLE BOOK OF

CRAP EXCUSES

Michael Powell

Michael O'Mara Humour

First published in Great Britain in 2001 by
Michael O'Mara Books Limited
9 Lion Yard
Tremadoc Road
London SW4 7NQ

A CIP catalogue record for this book is available from the British Library

ISBN 1–84317–040 –X

5 7 9 10 8 6 4

Designed and typeset by Design 23

Printed and bound in Great Britain by William Clowes, Beccles, Suffolk

CONTENTS

It's Easy

RULES FOR MAKING EXCUSES

Just because an excuse is rubbish doesn't mean you shouldn't use it.

Always base an excuse on the truth, unless you are a very good liar.

A good excuse saves a load of explanation.

You're never too old to learn a new excuse.

A bad excuse is better than nothing.

The better the excuse, the sooner it's over.

All excuses come to those who are late.

There is a time to speak and a time to make excuses.

Always put off today what you can excuse tomorrow.

One good excuse deserves another.

An excuse is its own reward.

Many excuses make light work.

No excuse like the first excuse.

A man without an excuse is but half a man.

Hello, Hello, Hello

LAW AND ORDER

Just pull over to the side of the road, sir...

I didn't know I was speeding. I must have nodded off.

I usually go much faster than this and I've never been stopped before.

Your headlights were blinding me. I was trying to get away.

My speedometer just broke.

My wife left me last week for a police officer, and I thought you were him trying to give her back!

I was speeding to waste petrol.

I wanted to send a message to OPEC that this country won't be held to ransom by rising oil prices.

I claim political asylum.

Why were you going that fast?

Have you ever tried to drive a car like this below eighty?

But my dog was driving!

I'm in a hurry, officer. Your wife is expecting me.

Yeah. I was speeding towards you. You looked like you could use some help.

The earth is travelling round the sun at over a hundred thousand miles per hour: what's an extra thirty?

I was getting a bag of crack cocaine out of the glove compartment when my gun fell off my lap and got jammed between the brake and accelerator pedals.

I lost my hamster this morning and I was hoping you would give me a full cavity search.

I thought it was OK to go ten over the speed limit.

THE FATHER OF ALL EXCUSES?
This is a confession a friend sent me – I would certainly never try this!

A couple of years ago in South Africa we attended a party one Saturday night. I'd had a few drinks already when a friend came running to me with my youngest son in his arms. The four-year-old had been found drinking a bottle of whisky. My wife and I had to rush him to hospital to get his stomach pumped. As I sped to hospital I drove into a police roadblock where they tested for drunk driving. I knew I was in trouble and didn't even bother to explain. I blew into their apparatus and it proved me legally drunk. I told the policeman that I didn't drink and that his apparatus must be faulty. He gave me another apparatus to blow in and I told my youngest to blow in the pipe. He also registered as being legally drunk. The policeman couldn't believe his eyes and let us go without further questions.

IT'S A FAIR COP...
Dumb criminal excuses

Two teenage joyriders in Florida were bailed after stealing their twenty-fifth car in two years. When they left the courthouse they immediately stole number twenty-six and crashed it less than an hour later. Their excuse was that they didn't have enough money for the bus fare home.

In Union, Kentucky, in 1993, two burglars were arrested after a failed house robbery. After they had ransacked the house, their car wouldn't start. So they went back inside and pleaded with the owner not to call the police. They even offered to put the stolen goods back and tidy up. Then they tried unsuccessfully to start their car a second time and asked the owner for a jump-start. When the police arrived, their excuse for the robbery was to get money to fix their car.

A death row inmate in Siberia strangled his cellmate, cut out his liver and boiled it in a metal mug. His excuse was that he wanted to avoid execution by pretending to be insane.

A Frenchman arrested for shooting his wife blamed a TV strike. 'There was nothing to look at. I was bored,' he said.

In 1987, an Australian was arrested for kicking his mother to death. His excuse: he had been listening to Bob Dylan's music.

In 1992, a sixteen-year-old boy was arrested for armed robbery of a jewellery store. His excuse: to get money to pay off his overdue library books.

EXCUSES FOR DIALLING 999
The following are real 999 calls made to the Metropolitan Police

Do you know a good stain remover?

There's a rat in my kitchen.

My bike was stolen last week.

I can't turn my tap off.

I think my neighbour is a spy.

I've found an umbrella. Where should I take it?

What time is it?

And Greater Manchester Police

Please send an officer to clear away some refuse sacks left behind by the binmen.

I've filled up my car with diesel instead of petrol. What should I do?

Could you tell me some train times please?

My road map has blown out of the car window – could you tell me where I am?

The emergency services are always extremely busy with genuine calls. Don't waste their time – engage your brain before you dial!

Do You Swear?

HOW TO AVOID JURY SERVICE

TWELVE JUST MEN
Or only eleven?
Getting out of jury service

Stand up, look over at the defendant and say confidently, 'Well, he looks guilty.'

Say that you're a professional psychic so you will know who is guilty even before the trial starts.

Plead a bladder problem. Declare that 'I will NOT serve unless I have a guarantee that I can pee every thirty minutes.'

Say 'I have a problem with this "sudden passion" thing. I once came in and found my husband/wife in bed with my neighbour. All I did was divorce him – I had no idea I could have shot him.'

Collapse in front of the court and pretend not to remember anything.

Tell the judge that you will make an excellent juror because you can spot guilty people immediately, then scream at him/her, 'You are guilty!'

Say, 'I'll listen to the evidence if I have to, but in my experience, ALL cops lie.'

Say, 'I have a problem keeping my mouth shut. Is it OK to participate in the objections?'

Say, 'I think the law is for sissies.'

Say, 'My religion bans me from sitting near other people.'

The End of the Affair

LOVE AND SEX

IMPOTENCE
It doesn't matter, I'm happy just to cuddle...

This is the first time this has happened to me today.

I guess it's just nature's way of saying 'no hard feelings'.

I'm suffering from Ascension Deficit Disorder.

I knew I shouldn't have given blood today.

I'm sorry, it seems to be set for Hillary, not Monica.

I guess my pointer just turned into a setter.

I'm turgidly challenged.

I'm saving myself for the match tomorrow.

I just spilled a bottle of fabric conditioner down my trousers.

I'm sorry, I can't imagine anyone I like right now.

I STILL LOVE YOU AS A FRIEND...
Breaking up with a partner

I guess I'm just not ready to commit.

I just need some space. I'm becoming an astronaut.

I just need some time. Can you come back in twenty years?

You deserve better.

It's me, not you.

The only thing we have in common is that we got married on the same day.

God loves me and I know he has a better life for me without you.

I'm holding you back.

I went through a past-life regression and it turns out that we were brother and sister in Ancient Egypt. So we can't see each other anymore. It would be incest.

I can't see you anymore. I have a detached retina.

I respect you too much. And I'm afraid you'd throw away all my back issues of *Hustler*, if you ever found them.

I'm married to my job.

I'd love to grow old with you, but you're too far in front for me to catch up.

We've drifted apart. I'll stay in the boat and you swim for help.

We're two different people. Actually, I'm three.

No, of course there's no one else. But if there was she'd have better tits than you.

I didn't know true happiness until I met you. And then it was too late.

OF COURSE I WANT TO SEE YOU...
Missing a date

The cat exploded and I had to take it to the vet.

I don't want to ruin our friendship.

I'm not your type. I'm not inflatable.

I'm washing my hair on Friday night, so I can't see you. Saturday? Well, it's got to dry hasn't it?

I don't date outside my own species.

IS THAT THE TIME?
Ways to end a bad date

Wow. That's amazing. I like watching TV too.

How many kids shall we have?

Would you like to hear your name in Klingon?

Sorry, I'm a little preoccupied. I'm expecting a call.
My wife could go into labour at any moment.

I've really matured. Last year I'd never have
bothered with someone who looks like you.

I love cats, too. How do you like to cook them?

The alarm on my watch has gone off. Does that mean it's time for my medication or yours?

Most of the voices in my head really like you! It's been really nice, but I have to scream now.

Can we stop at the clinic? I need to pick up some results.

Let's get the bill. The Viagra will be wearing off soon.

I've been wanting to date you since I read about you on a toilet wall last year.

I can't wait to show you some of the sex tricks I learned in prison.

...so now I've just got one big nostril. Can I borrow your mirror?

...and so by touching your hand I am able to make a complete replica...

Boy, there's lots of skin on you. I should be able to finish that sewing project tonight.

My mission on your planet is nearing its conclusion.

My three favourite hobbies are meeting people, power tools and unblocking my drains.

I have a uterus in a jar at home. Would you like to see it?

I'd Love to but...

I'M BUSY

I'D LOVE TO BUT...

I have to stay at home to rearrange my sock drawer.

My grandmother got her arm caught in a microwave.

I wish I could but I have to stay home and mend my canoe.

I can't because I have to tickle my llama to keep it alive.

I have to wax my cat.

I'll have to check with the Mother Ship.

None of my socks match.

I can't, my cat's depressed and I have to stay home.

There are important world issues that need worrying about.

I have an appointment with God.

I only have one shoe on!

I'm not stupid, I just choose not to pay attention.

The penguins stole my sanity!

Work. Work. Work

AT THE OFFICE

IT'S MORE THAN MY JOB'S WORTH...

We don't know how to do that.

It's too late to do that today. Come back
tomorrow after 5 p.m.

The person who deals with that is on sabbatical.

It isn't cost effective.

I'm new.

I'm new.
(Said by the same person seven months later.)

I'm not authorized to tell you.

Our computer system is down/being replaced/being delivered tomorrow.

You've reached the wrong department.

We've lost your file – you don't exist.

It's Tuesday.

A PATHETIC EXCUSE FOR A CAT?

An American woman had missed a lot of work and her boss made her promise she would not be late, but on the first day back she woke to find her cat bleeding. The poor cat had a hole in its belly where an abscess had burst.

The vet was very accommodating and wrote her an official excuse, which hung on the boss's noticeboard for a *very* long time.

It read, 'Please excuse Miss X for being late in to work today. Her cat had a hole in it.'

LATE FOR WORK

First of all, define what you mean by late.

I lost the instructions for my alarm clock.

I got lost in thought. It was unfamiliar territory and I took an hour to find directions.

My car doors were frozen shut and I had to wait for the sun to thaw them out.

The car got stuck in reverse and I had to back all the way here.

I'm awake and dressed. What more do you want?

I was putting on my trousers and my head got stuck in the toilet.

My dog ate the car keys and I had to wait for him to take a dump to get them back.

I stopped to help an old lady across the road but she was really a man in drag. He pulled me into some bushes and beat the crap out of me. Then he said he was sorry and wouldn't stop crying and apologizing. So I took him for a coffee and tried to talk through some of his issues. It's good policy for employees to reach out to the community and help other fellow travellers on life's journey…rich tapestry…blah, blah, blah…

It was a really hot day, causing the molecules on the surface of the road to expand, with a significant resultant increase in the distance between my home and work.

I'm not late. I just thought I'd turn up early for tomorrow.

I overslept and dreamed that my job sucked, the pay was lousy and that you were an asshole.

It took me longer than usual to get the nipple clamps off.

I was looking up the word gastroenteritis in the dictionary.

I have a morbid fear of making left turns, so I had to drive to the end of the motorway.

THE SPIRIT IS WILLING...
Missing work altogether

My wife was having sex and I wanted to be there.

I was building a thermonuclear detonator.

I was recovering from foot surgery: yours in my arse.

I couldn't find a parking space, so I had to turn around and drive all the way home.

I won the lottery and now you work for me. You're fired.

I had to change out of my superhero costume after a busy night of fighting crime and I couldn't find my civvies.

I won't be in today – my hair won't start.

I have a TV, a vibrator and pizza delivery. Why should I leave home?

I've found a better job. Serving fast food.

I thought this was my year off.

Don't give me your attitude. I have one of my own.

My head fell off. No, seriously! Don't you believe me? You want me to bring it in?

When I got up this morning, I washed down my Prozac with a litre of prune juice. Now I can't leave the toilet, but I feel good about it.

I was picking my nose and I pierced my nasal septum and just kind of kept on going. I think I scratched my brain.

I can't come to work today because I'm stalking my previous boss who fired me for not showing up. OK pal?

My wife's breasts are sore after her operation, so I have to stay home and massage them.

My husband's balls are really swollen after his vasectomy, so I have to stay home to keep them gently cupped.

The four-armed fisting monkey just escaped from the zoo. The police are advising everyone to stay indoors today.

I can't come to work today. I am too busy cutting the ears off my hostages.

My mother-in-law has come back as one of the living dead and I have to track her down and drive a stake through her heart. One day should nail it.

I have eye problems. I can't see myself coming into work today.

I have too many issues and I don't want them to affect my performance at work.

The voices told me to clean all the guns today.

My stigmata is acting up again.

I have twenty-four-hour projectile leprosy ... but I'll definitely be in tomorrow.

Constipation has made me a walking time bomb.

I just found out that I was switched at birth. It would be irresponsible and illegal for me to come to work knowing that my employee records now contain false information ...

My therapist is very pleased with my progress. He says the hockey mask and straitjacket are just temporary measures and I'll have the report on your desk by four o'clock.

I seem to have come down with Attention Deficit Disorder and what about that game last night so that if I cut along the dotted lines and I still can't open the tin I'll make sure you're the first to know when I decide to switch to gas but thank you for calling.

SLEEP? WORK? SLEEP? WORK?
Caught snoozing at work

They warned me at the blood bank this might happen.

I'm taking a power nap. They recommended it on that time management course you sent me on.

If you paid me more, I might be able to stay awake.

I was working smarter not harder.

How can I work efficiently if you keep disturbing my sleep?

I was testing the keyboard for drool resistance.

This is in return for the six hours I lay awake last night worrying about work.

Damn it. If you hadn't interrupted me, I'd nearly worked out a solution to our biggest problem.

I love my work so much that I'm saving all of it for later.

I don't know what your problem is but I bet it's hard to pronounce.

… Amen.

I'm on a Stress Level Elimination Exercise Plan (SLEEP).

Someone must've put decaf in the wrong pot.

Boy, that cold medicine I took last night just won't wear off!

Ah, the unique and unpredictable circadian rhythms of the workaholic!

Wasn't sleeping. Was trying to pick up contact lens without hands.

LEAVING ALREADY?
Excuses to get off early.

I have to get my big toe calibrated.

I'm going on a date with a sadomasochistic necrophile.

I'm having my hats checked this afternoon.

I have to stand in a long line for no good reason, while petty bureaucrats take inordinate amounts of time to work out the tiny problems that they detect in perfectly routine transactions.

The pharaoh is acting up; there's going to be a terrible rain of frogs.

I have to have my waistband let out

My biological clock is ticking.

My hair aches.

My truss snapped.

A friend of mine is being reincarnated and I have to go to the zoo.

I need to check out the hole in the ozone layer.

I'm breaking in my shoes.

Get 'em Young

KIDS, DON'T YOU JUST...

A NOTE FROM YOUR MOTHER
A list of real excuses written by parents on their children's sick notes

Please excuse James from being absent on June 28, 29, 30, 31, 32 and also 33.

Please excuse Robbie from being. It was his father's fault.

Please excuse Jane. She is having trouble with her ovals.

Richard has been away because he has had two teeth taken off his face.

My son is under the doctor and should not take fizical ed. Please execute him.

Please excuse Joanna from being at school yesterday. She was in bed with gramps.

Please excuse Roland from P.E. for a few days. Yesterday he fell out of a tree and misplaced his hip.

Lee was absent yesterday because he was playing football. He was hit in his growing part.

Alison won't be at school a week from Monday. We have to go to her funeral.

I kept Rachel home because she had to go Christmas shopping because I don't know what size she wear.

My daughter was absent yesterday because she spent the weekend with the Marines and was exhausted.

Please excuse Eloise for being absent. She was sick and I had her shot.

Please excuse Veronica from Jim today. She is administrating.

Victoria could not come to school today because she has been bothered by very close veins.

Andrew will not be in school cus he has an acre in his side.

Please excuse Roy from school. He has very loose vowels.

Please excuse Fred for being absent yesterday. He had diarrhoea and his boots leak.

Louis was absent yesterday because he missed his bust.

Please excuse Annabel for missing school yesterday. We forgot to get the Sunday paper off the doormat, and when we found it on Monday, we thought it was Sunday.

Please excuse Jamie for being absent yesterday. He had a cold and could not breed well.

Olivia was absent yesterday as she was having a gangover.

Maryann was absent for five days because she had a fever, sore throat, headache and upset stomach. Her sister was also sick, fever and sore throat, her brother had a low grade fever and ached all over. I wasn't the best either, sore throat and fever. There must be something going around, her father even got hot last night.

List attributed to Nisheeth Parekh,
University of Texas Medical Branch, Galveston

WE'LL SEE...
Parents to children

We didn't have them when we were your age.

You can have/do/eat it when you're older/taller.

If you'd just told me the truth in the first place...

I left my wallet in another time zone.

EXCUSE FOR MISSING GEOGRAPHY LESSONS?

A woman called to make reservations at a travel agency in America.

'I want to go from Chicago to Hippopotamus, New York.'

The agent was at a loss for words. Finally, the agent said: 'Are you sure that's the name of the town?'

'Yes, what flights do you have?' replied the customer.

After some searching, the agent came back with, 'I'm sorry, ma'am, I've looked up every airport code in the country and can't find a Hippopotamus anywhere.'

The customer retorted, 'Oh don't be silly. Everyone knows where it is. Check your map!'

The agent scoured a map of the state of New York and finally offered, 'You don't mean Buffalo, do you?'

'That's it! I knew it was a big animal!'

STEEP LEARNING CURVE

Two cocky straight-A students missed an important Monday test after a weekend of wild partying. They sloped into college on the Tuesday and were allowed to re-sit the test that afternoon after explaining to their professor that they had driven away for the weekend and got stranded after blowing a tyre. That afternoon, they sat the test, in separate rooms, each smugly congratulating themselves for their cleverness. They opened the test paper and had no problems answering the first question, which was worth five marks. But when they turned the page they found just one other question, worth ninety-five marks. The question: 'Which tyre?'

PLEASE MISS...

I bumped into Shania Twain last night and she thought my essay would be a really good song, so she took it, and will be returning it soon.

Sorry I was late to school. When I got up this morning, my medulla oblongata just felt really funny.

Homework? I was supposed to bring it back to school? I thought it stayed at home.

I was studying nicely when a herd of rampaging bees ran me over, and bit me.

I was jumped by Jehovah witnesses who ran off with my homework.

I was late into school today because I was accosted by several heavily armed dwarves who felt vengeful about their lack of stature.

I was late because there are eight kids in my family, and my mother set the alarm for seven.

I am late for religious reasons. I have recently converted to Hinduism and there was a cow in the road.

EXCUSES FOR NOT KNOWING THE ANSWER

– Various authorities agree…
means: I overheard someone saying this in class.

– It is a well-established theory…
means: I can't remember where I found it.

– The implications are clear…
means: The implications are not clear to me,
or I would have said what they are.

– This experiment has left many questions
unanswered…
means: I didn't find anything out of any
significance.

A Moment on the Lips

DIET CHEATS

EAT THEN CHEAT

If you eat something in secret, it has no calories.

If you have a diet drink with any other food, the calories are cancelled out by the diet drink.

When you are eating with someone else, if they eat more than you do then your calories don't count.

Food used for medicinal reasons doesn't count, such as brandy, honey, ice cream and chocolate cake.

When you eat food at the cinema, the calories don't count because they are part of the entertainment.

Food licked off knives and spoons when cooking has no calories.

Food has to have calories to be fattening. Calories are a measure of heat, so eating frozen food, like ice cream, will actually make you lose weight.

Any food eaten after you have just weighed yourself doesn't count.

SAVE POUNDS!!

Use cheap scales because they always weigh half a stone lighter.

Never weigh with wet hair.

Go to the toilet first.

Take all your clothes off; remove glasses, body jewellery, make-up and prosthetics; cut your nails, squeeze your spots, cut your hair, shave your legs and clean your ears.

Raise your hands above your head to make you lighter.

Breathe out!

MORE DIET CHEATS

But the doughnut was calling my name.

Foods that are the same colour have the same number of calories. Examples are: spinach and pistachio ice cream; mushrooms and white chocolate. NOTE: Chocolate is a universal colour and may be substituted for any other food colour.

Chocolate has many preservatives. Preservatives make you look younger.

Eat off someone else's plate. The calories don't count if it's not your food.

I'm not overweight, I'm undertall!

Doctor, Doctor

MEDICAL MATTERS

DOCTOR, DOCTOR!

On 7 September 1999, a doctor in America ended a successful Caesarean section with a bizarre act that landed him with a five million-dollar lawsuit and the nickname 'Dr Zorro'. Witnesses in the operating theatre allege that he carved his initials, 'A' and 'Z' on the woman's stomach in letters three inches high. He is said to have excused himself at the time with the words: 'I did such a beautiful job, I'll initial it.' The doctor's licence has been suspended.

KINKY

When, in December 1996, a thirty-two-year-old man from Kentucky shot himself in the left shoulder with a .22-calibre rifle, he told paramedics it was 'to see how it felt'. He did the same again a year later because it 'felt so good' the last time, he just had to do it again.

TOP TEN EXCUSES TO USE WHEN PRESENTING YOURSELF AT A HOSPITAL WITH A VEGETABLE LODGED UP YOUR BACKSIDE

I was just cleaning some vegetables in the shower when . . .

I was just digging on my allotment when there was a solar eclipse . . .

I was walking past the vegetable section in the supermarket when I slipped and . . .

I was attacked in the park by an 8-foot rabbit. He did some bad things, doctor.

My teeth hurt so I haven't been chewing my food properly for a while now.

I'm very absent-minded. I meant to put it in the fridge.

There was this chutney recipe. I was just following the instructions.

My dog . . .

I was kidnapped by aliens. They took me up to their mother ship and did lots of tests. My memory is very hazy. I think you'd better take a look . . .

I was sunbathing naked in the garden when a bunch of kids started throwing vegetables over the fence.

FIVE EXCUSES TO USE WHEN PRESENTING YOURSELF AT A HOSPITAL WITH A WINE BOTTLE LODGED UP YOUR BACKSIDE

I was just opening a bottle of wine in the shower when . . .

I lost my corkscrew.

I practise tantric meditation and I was trying out a new posture.

I was the guest of honour at the launch of an ocean liner. Well, the Dom Perignon sort of glanced off the hull and . . .

A mate told me that you can't beat the feeling of sticking a bottle up your arse.

SO EMBARRASSING IT HAS TO BE TRUE ...

A colleague called in one Monday morning to report that he wouldn't be in that day. Apparently he'd accompanied his girlfriend – for moral support you understand – while she had her tongue pierced. Obviously the girlfriend was made of sterner stuff than my colleague, so when the talk turned to the piercing of other body parts our hero began to feel a little faint, and went outside to take a few deep breaths. Unfortunately, his squeamishness got the better of him and he passed out cold on the pavement. He ended up being taken to casualty by his girlfriend – for moral support you understand – to have six staples put in the back of his head. We're convinced he was fit to work on the Monday, but was too embarrassed . . .

It was an Accident

INSURANCE CLAIMS

IT JUST CAME OUT OF NOWHERE ...
Real car insurance claims

The other vehicle collided with mine without giving any warning of its intentions.

I started to slow down but the traffic was more stationary than I thought.

My car was legally parked as it backed into the other car.

The old man was all over the road. I had to swerve several times before I hit him.

Trying to kill a fly, I drove into a telegraph pole.

I thought my window was down, but realized it wasn't when my head went through it.

Returning home, I drove into the wrong house and hit a tree I haven't got.

I had been driving for forty years when I fell asleep at the wheel and crashed the car.

I was going at about 70 or 80 m.p.h. when my girlfriend on the pillion reached over and grabbed my testicles so I lost control.

The indirect cause of the accident was a little man in a small car with a big mouth.

I moved away from the kerb, looked at my mother-in-law and drove over the embankment.

To avoid hitting the car in front, I struck the pedestrian.

IT WASN'T MY FAULT!
More car insurance claims

I pulled into a lay-by with smoke coming from under the bonnet. I realised the car was on fire so took my dog and smothered it with a blanket.

An invisible car appeared from nowhere, hit my car and vanished.

On the M6 I moved from the centre lane to the fast lane but the other car didn't give way.

A truck backed through my windscreen into my wife's face.

I was sure that the old man would never reach the other side of the road, when I struck him.

I had one eye on a parked car, another on approaching lorries, and another on the woman behind.

I told the police officer that I was unhurt, but upon removing my helmet discovered I had a fractured skull.

I had been shopping for plants all day and was returning home. As I reached a junction a hedge sprang up, obscuring my view, and I did not see the other vehicle.

I was driving to the doctor with rear end trouble when my universal joint gave way, causing me to crash.

On approach to the traffic lights the car in front suddenly broke.

ME OFFICER?
Yet more car insurance claims

The pedestrian couldn't decide which direction to run, so I ran him over.

As I approached an intersection a sign suddenly appeared in a place where no stop sign had ever been before. I could not stop in time to avoid the accident.

I didn't think the speed limit applied after midnight.

I saw a slow-moving, sad-faced old gentleman as he bounced off the front of my car.

The telephone pole was approaching. I was attempting to swerve out of the way when I struck the front end.

I started to turn and it was at this point I noticed a camel and an elephant tethered at the verge. This distraction caused me to lose concentration and hit a bollard.

I was on my way to see an unconscious patient who had convulsions and was blocked by a tanker.

No witnesses would admit having seen the mishap until after it happened.

First car stopped suddenly, second car hit first car and a haggis ran into the rear of second car.

The car in front hit the pedestrian but he got up so I hit him again.

We had completed the turn and had just straightened the car when Miss X put her foot down hard and headed for the ladies' loo.

Spin 'til You're Dizzy

POLITICS

YOU'VE NEVER HAD IT SO GOOD
Politicians' excuses and lies – what they really mean...

WE HAVE NO QUARREL WITH THEIR PEOPLE...
We will bomb the suckers until the crazy guy with the moustache has no one left to rule.

WE HAVE NO ALTERNATIVE BUT TO USE FORCE.
Let's try out these new smart bombs.

COLLATERAL DAMAGE WAS KEPT TO A MINIMUM.
The Chinese embassy was just too shiny to ignore.

WE MUST NOT INTERFERE IN THIS DELICATE
MATTER.
This country doesn't produce any oil.

THIS COUNTRY WILL NOT BE HELD TO RANSOM
BY PUBLIC OPINION.
Democracy sucks.

IT IS NOT IN THE PUBLIC INTEREST.
If anyone finds out, we're screwed.

THERE IS NO RISK TO PUBLIC HEALTH.
See you next year. I'll be in my bunker.

IT WAS AN ERROR OF JUDGEMENT.
. . . and if it wasn't for you pesky kids I'd never
have been caught. Can I have my job back now?

TALKS WERE SUBSTANTIVE.
OK, we've agreed on deep crust pepperoni, but
the chicken wings are non-negotiable.

THAT IS NOT FOR ME TO SAY.
I haven't been briefed on this bit.

IT IS EVERY CITIZEN'S RIGHT . . .
We can afford that.

STATISTICALLY, IT IS STILL A VERY SAFE MEANS
OF TRANSPORT.
Cancel my ticket, I'm walking.

IT WAS A VERY HUMBLING EXPERIENCE.
It was squalid and depressing.

WITH RESPECT . . .
Do you want some or what? Don't mess with me, asshole. I know where you live.

I LISTENED WITH INTEREST.
I was so bored I nearly chewed my arm off.

I AM NOT GOING TO PRE-EMPT THE REPORT.
I haven't had a chance to bribe the judge yet.

THERE HAS BEEN NO BREACH OF NATIONAL SECURITY.
What do you mean they stole *all* the passwords?

A WEEK IS A LONG TIME IN POLITICS.
My mind's gone blank. Say something, quick...

SOMETIMES POLITICIANS HAVE TO MAKE TOUGH DECISIONS.
If you all put your money in this bag and lie face down on the floor, no one will get hurt.

THAT'S WHY I BECAME A POLITICIAN.
…apart from the power, status, casual sex and diplomatic immunity.

THAT IS FOR THE ELECTORATE TO DECIDE.
We don't have a policy yet.

WE LISTEN TO THEIR OPINIONS.
It's a marginal seat.

WE TAKE THIS MATTER VERY SERIOUSLY INDEED.
Next time, we'll make damn sure no one finds out.

DID THEY REALLY THINK THESE WOULD WORK?
They said (allegedly)...

The streets are safe in Philadelphia; it's only the people that make them unsafe.
FORMER PHILADELPHIA MAYOR AND POLICE CHIEF FRANK RIZZO

The President has kept all of the promises he intended to keep.
CLINTON AIDE GEORGE STEPHANOPOULOS SPEAKING ON *LARRY KING LIVE*

Without censorship, things can get terribly confused in the public mind.
GENERAL WILLIAM WESTMORELAND

It isn't pollution that's harming the environment. It's impurities in our air and water that are doing it.
FORMER US VICE PRESIDENT DAN QUAYLE

Outside of the killings, Washington has one of the lowest crime rates in the country.
MAYOR MARION BARRY, WASHINGTON, DC

I haven't committed a crime. What I did was fail to comply with the law.
DAVID DINKINS, NEW YORK CITY MAYOR

I was under medication when I made the decision to burn the tapes.
RICHARD NIXON, US PRESIDENT

We are not without accomplishment. We have managed to distribute poverty equally.
NGUYEN CO THATCH, VIETNAMESE FOREIGN MINISTER

We don't necessarily discriminate. We simply exclude certain types of people.
COLONEL GERALD WELLMAN, ROYAL OFFICER TRAINING CORPS INSTRUCTOR

I've always thought that underpopulated countries in Africa are vastly under-polluted.
LAWRENCE SUMMERS, CHIEF ECONOMIST OF THE WORLD BANK, ON THE ISSUE OF EXPORTING TOXIC WASTE TO THE THIRD WORLD

In any country there must be people who have to die. They are the sacrifices any nation has to make to achieve law and order.
IDI AMIN

When the President does it that means it is not illegal.
RICHARD NIXON, US PRESIDENT

Sometimes democracy must be bathed in blood.
AUGUSTO PINOCHET

We are not retreating – we are advancing in another direction.
GENERAL DOUGLAS MACARTHUR

Fit as a Fiddle

UP, ONE, TWO, THREE

FIT FOR LIFE? FIT FOR NOTHING...
Here are some excuses doctors and physical therapists heard from patients, explaining why they can't exercise

An earthquake drained my pool.

My dog ate my running shoes.

I can't exercise because of the grizzly bear. (Heard near a popular walking path in Anchorage, Alaska.)

My wife would be angry with me if I lost weight.

If I exercise, I might not have enough energy left over for sex.

I can't because of the volcanic ash.

The TV at the gym is always on something I don't want to watch.

It's Only a Game

SPORTS

WE WAS ROBBED...
Sport

It was like being in a foreign country.
IAN RUSH ON THE DIFFICULTY OF PLAYING ABROAD

We actually got the winner three minutes from the end but then they equalized.
IAN MCNAIL

Sure there have been injuries and deaths in boxing – but none of them serious.
ALAN MINTER

People think we make $3 million and $4 million a year. They don't realize that most of us only make $500,000.
PETE INCAVIGLIA, BASEBALL PLAYER

Golfing Goofs

I hit my stomach during the swing.

I play better when I can hit the ball.

The air is very heavy today.

That shot would have been perfect if it hadn't hit the tree.

The ball must have hit a low-pressure air pocket.

If I had some of Tiger Woods' money, I'd be able to buy a decent set of clubs, too.

It would have been a birdie if the ball hadn't stopped.

I'm wearing my sensible trousers today.

Football Own Goals

The goalkeeper obstructed my view of the goal.

I don't play well on a Sunday.

I'm saving myself for the final.

I was too busy kicking spectators.

I don't believe in training. It destroys spontaneity.

I had a kebab half an hour ago and I still feel like I'm dragging a ten-pound turd around in my stomach.

I don't have my lucky earrings on today.

Rugby

It was a choice between his head and the ball, so I kicked the one with less hair.

He snatched the ball off me, splashing me with mud, so then I got really mad...

Weightlifting

You mean that crack cocaine cut with bull semen isn't a cure for the flu?

Long Jump

Whad'ya mean 'no jump'? I didn't just leap twenty-two feet for fun you know.

Curling

I forgot my lucky broom.

High Jump

I'm taller in the morning.

Boxing

He kept hitting me, so I bit his ear off.

Rowing

Sure we sank. But there was so much water out there.

Horse Racing
I stopped for the photo finish.

Skiing

I didn't expect it to snow today.

Diving

I banged my head on the board, and then I lost a kidney when I belly-flopped, but I don't think anybody noticed.

Judo

He tried to trip me up. That's against the rules, isn't it?

Fencing

He lunged at me with his sword, so I had no choice but to shoot him.

American Wrestling

I guess I just shouldn't have lain on the floor for ten minutes rubbing my leg, waiting for the other guy to jump off the ropes.

Chess

Someone must have programmed that computer to beat me.

Darts

I throw better when there's a tail wind.

Snooker

I forgot my lucky chalk.

Table Tennis

My opponent's shoes keep squeaking.

Tennis

I don't play my best game on grass. I'm more comfortable hitting a ball against the garage door.

Cricket

I was put off when someone in the crowd sat up with interest.

Leaves on the Line

TRANSPORT

THE NEXT TRAIN ON PLATFORM *CRACKLE* IS THE DELAYED *SQUAWK* TO *CCCRRRRR* ... OH I GIVE UP. TAXI!!

Real excuses given to passengers for late or cancelled trains

I'm ever so sorry. We've run out of fuel.

The wrong kind of weather.

A 34 per cent increase in delays due to increasing suicides.

We are not removing the buddleia fast enough.

We have to do more.

The wrong kind of snow.

Fleas in the driver's cab.

The wrong kind of leaves.

We didn't stop at the last scheduled station because of skiddy tracks.

The service is delayed today because the driver is only five feet one and his swivel chair has broken. He's too short to reach the pedals.

The driver is still eating his sandwiches.

There was a problem with the rostering. The driver is sunning himself on the Algarve and there is no one else to drive the train.

We've got a problem with rabbits and have to keep an eye on their burrowing … rabbit warrens have already added to the instability of cuttings and caused a landslide after a flash flood.

I apologise for the delay but the computer controlling the signalling has the Monday Morning Blues.

And I Said to God

to God

BIBLICAL EXCUSES

BIBLICAL EXCUSES

*That's a nice story, but now tell me where
you've really been for the last three days.*
JONAH'S MOTHER

It was bit muddy.
WHY MOSES WAS RELUCTANT TO CROSS THE RED SEA

You can't get the wood these days.
WHY ABRAHAM DIDN'T SACRIFICE ISAAC

She made me do it!
ADAM, ON WHY HE SPENT EVERY SATURDAY OUT
SHOPPING FOR CLOTHES AFTER BEING CAST OUT OF THE
GARDEN OF EDEN

I didn't know it was going to be so loud!
JOSHUA, AFTER THE WALLS OF JERICHO CAME
TUMBLING DOWN

I was really bored.
GOD'S EXCUSE FOR THE SEVEN PLAGUES OF EGYPT

*Sorry about the myrrh – they didn't have any
teddy bears.*
BALTHAZAR

Dinosaurs? What dinosaurs?
NOAH

The Devil makes work for idle hands.
GOD ON THE CREATION OF WOMAN

I didn't know my own strength.
SAMSON

I'm not eating that – it's not kosher.
A LION, ON SEEING DANIEL

I didn't say kill the infants. I said kill the ants!
HEROD

He started it!
CAIN, ON ABEL

Sorry, Goliath, I didn't know it was loaded.
DAVID

I had a puncture.
THE PRODIGAL SON

Brought to Book

OVERDUE AT THE LIRARY

LONG OVERDUE?
What to say to avoid those overdue library book fines...

I took it to my girlfriend's house, but we've since had a bit of a falling out, and I can't get it back because of the restraining order... I could maybe ask the police to get it?

I took that book out months ago. Why are you bothering me about it now?

My little sister puked on it.

I have a bad back, and can't carry it here because it's so heavy.

For Every Occasion

FOR EVERY OCCASION...

Some big kids made me do it.

Sex isn't everything.

I was just following orders.

This has nothing to do with my mother.

At this time I am unable to process your order for the new CPU for your computer as our computers are down.

This is definitely a shortcut.

I could tell you, but then I'd have to kill you.

I have a high metabolism.

I was away that day.

Your Honour, I stabbed my wife in the back twenty-five times to hide her suicide from our son.

Trust me. I do this all the time.

Bring it back if you don't like it.

The cheque's in the post.

The author and the publishers would like to thank all those who submitted material to our regular humour e-mail address:
jokes@michaelomara books.com
We always welcome new contributions, but regret that space does not allow for individual credits.

The Little Book of Totally Stupid Men – ISBN 1-85479-833-2
The Little Book of Despair – ISBN 1-85479-818-9
The Little Book of Tantric Sex for Busy People –
   ISBN 1-85479-685-2
The Little Book of Sex Fantasies – ISBN 1-85479-725-5

The Little Book of Minge Topiary – ISBN 1-84317-051-5 (£2.99)

New, expanded 128-page editions.
All at £2.50 each including postage (UK only).

The Little Book of Farting – ISBN 1-85479-445-0
The Little Book of Stupid Men – ISBN 1-85479-454-X
The Little Toilet Book – ISBN 1-85479-456-6
The Little Book of Cockney Rhyming Slang – 1-84317-027-2
The Little Book of Crap Excuses – ISBN 1-84317-040-X
The Little Book of Crap Advice – ISBN 1-84317-041-8
LUVTLK! ltle bk of luv txt – ISBN 1-84317-042-6
Dirty Cockney Rhyming Slang – ISBN 1-84317-035-3
The Little Book of Speed Dating – ISBN 1-84317-074-4
The Little Book of Dirty Speed Dating – ISBN 1-84317-080-9
WAN2TLK? ltle bk of txt msgs – ISBN 1-84317-082-5

All Michael O'Mara titles are available by post from:

Bookpost, PO Box 29, Douglas, Isle of Man IM99 1BQ

Credit cards accepted.

Telephone: 01624-677237
Fax: 01624-670923
E-mail: bookshop@enterprise.net
Internet: www.bookpost.co.uk
Free postage and packing in the UK.